No Place To Be Me

A View From A Federal Prison Camp

William Moorehead

TO: LEANNE
FROM Bill

The story, experiences, and ideas are the author's alone. Events are portrayed to the best of William Moorehead's memory. While all the stories here are true, some names and identifying details have been changed to protect the privacy of the people involved.

Cover design by Delaney-Designs.com.
Photo by Greg, Inc. dba Davis Digital Services

Special thanks to Tammy Letherer for her editing expertise and time that she spent to help me complete this book. I am grateful.

ISBN-13:
978-1540648938

ISBN-10:
1540648931

DEDICATION

I dedicate this book to my sons Timothy, Donald, Jimmie, William, and Maurice who showed nothing but love and respect throughout this period in my life. Also to my sister Maggie who always wrote me those encouraging letters, and to my sister Laura and her family who came from St. Louis to visit me on several occasions. To Mia, a special thanks for your visits and financial support every month for three years so I could buy food that was edible.

I also dedicate this book to all the people who prayed for me and you know who you are. I can tell you that I felt your prayers.

To Rob and Bridgett, Darren and Kurt, your visits always lifted my spirits.

I say thanks be to the Lord who never left me. It was the Grace of God that got me through this.

CONTENTS

Pride goes before destruction,

a haughty spirit before a fall.

Proverbs 16:18

INTRODUCTION

This is not the book I wanted to write.

I began writing a book about my life in Mississippi during the 1940's, 50's, and part of the 60's. Then circumstances in my life changed. I was sentenced to four years in a federal prison camp in Marion, Illinois. Even though I had hoped to write a book about growing up, I was living a different story and I could not get away from it. I prayed, waited for the answer, and it came to me: I was to write this instead.

This book is not a feel-good kind of book, but I hope it's a book that will give you a peek into a correctional system that is out of control and in much need of repair, reorganization, and change.

I ended up serving three years of my sentence in a prison camp. A camp is a minimum security institution that has dormitory housing and limited or no fencing. I had the freedom and opportunity to meet and to talk with other inmates who had served their time at other types of prisons and I have included some of their thoughts in addition to mine.

This book is not a detailed working of the penal system. Hopefully it will spur someone to take a deeper look at what works and what doesn't work. One of the things I hope to do is shine a light on how one gets into this system, who they are, how they cope, what they become, and where they go after release.

According to a 2008 study conducted by the Pew Center, when I served my time I was one of 2,319,158 adults being held in all state and federal prisons or jails. That meant that more than one in every 100 adults was incarcerated. These 2008 figures were 25,000 greater than just one year before. By 2016, according to the Bureau of Prisons (BOP), the federal prison population alone was 192,170 and the average sentence length was 9.9 years, with most of those inmates (53%) serving sentences for drug trafficking offenses.

The 2016 national recidivism rate is more than 55% and remains virtually unchanged, with a majority of the young prisoners that are released returning to jail or prison within three years. In my conversations with some of the younger men, I discovered that being in jail didn't seem to bother them. In fact, some saw it as a status symbol because once they return to the streets they are admired by younger guys for the way they dress or talk.

From what I observed, the system works differently for different people; it seemed to be operated and controlled by people who had no intention of being fair. An example of this is plea bargaining. Ninety-five percent of all criminal court cases are settled by some type of plea agreement, which means that you give up your basic rights, including the right to a trial. If you're not willing to implicate someone, you will not likely get a good deal. But if you do give someone up and go to prison, you become a person who can't be trusted and will be labeled as a snitch. Is this justice, to get a conviction in any way possible, whether right or wrong?

There are some groups, like The Sentencing Project, that are working to change things within the system. But change is difficult because it involves politics, and most politicians do not want to appear to be soft on crime.

To set the record straight, I've always preferred speaking over writing. People have told me that I write as though I am angry. In this case, I am not angry because I went to prison. I believe I have overcome my incarceration experience. But I am angry at what this system does to people.

I used to be one of those who totally believed in the justice system. I believed that if a person did something wrong he should be locked up, even though my oldest son and brother have been in the prison system for years because of drug issues. I did not have sympathy for people caught up in the system because I thought they were bad guys who deserved to be put away. Now I know that there are a lot of good people who should not be in prison. Having been on the inside has given me a totally different viewpoint. I've learned the ugly truth about this system, beginning from the time I was charged until I left prison, and even when I was back in society trying to rebuild my life. And I know from my conversations with many other men that my struggles were not unique.

But I violated the law. And I believe it was God's will that I went to prison, not only to pay for my crime, but also because of who and what I had become. God gave me three years to get myself together.

Who do I blame for having been in prison? I blame myself. Who do I blame for this broken, messed-up system? I blame the people who created and operate the system and that includes a lot of people.

1 THE BEGINNING

I grew up in Mississippi during the 1950's and 60's in a large family of six girls and three boys. We lived on a plantation nine miles north of the small town Greenwood. In those days, the only job opportunities we had were working in the cotton fields. When you live on a farm, it's a family affair, so all of us worked; I started in the fields at the age of six. Even from this early age I knew that I did not want to make farming a career.

Since we were sharecroppers, we got paid according to the number of bales of cotton we picked. In late spring and early summer we chopped the cotton and in late summer and early fall we picked it. The cotton had to be picked before we could start school, which meant that we started late each year, in October, and dropped out every May to return to the fields. This was typical for most black farm families, and I learned early how to play catch up.

One night this all ended when I awoke to the sound of gunshots. It was around midnight, and my oldest sister Adell came running through the house crying and shouting, "Wake up! Wake up! Mama just shot Daddy."

My sister Willola told her to go back to bed. "Mama is in Chicago," she said. Our mother, Ophelia, had gone to Chicago that winter to work and earn money to pay for a car my parents had bought. What we didn't know was that she had come home early and was waiting for my father with a 12-gauge shotgun. When he came home with another woman, there was a confrontation and he tried to take the gun. It went off and he was shot.

We all rushed outside but my older sisters pushed me and my three younger siblings back so we couldn't see the body. All I remember was hearing my mother crying in the yard until the county sheriff came and took her away. I was old enough to understand that my father was dead, but I didn't understand why.

I wouldn't say that I come from a broken home, but rather a shattered home, because the pieces could not be put back together. My mother was charged with murder and sent off to prison. All nine of us children were divided up and sent to live with different relatives. I stayed, along with two of my sisters, with Adell, who was just 17 but was suddenly responsible for the three of us. In rural Mississippi in the 1950s there were no social workers or child protection services to check on us or to stop Adell from taking us to live somewhere else, so we moved across the state. My older brother went to live with an aunt, and my other siblings went to our grandmother. With so many miles between us and no car, we had to rely on other people to take us to see each other. For the next three years, I saw my siblings about once every six months.

I suppose I grew up angry about the whole thing, but I didn't know who to blame. I couldn't blame my mother because I loved her too much and I just couldn't see any wrong in her. She was the most important person in my life. Until that point I had been a happy child and I thought we had a happy family. Suddenly, all I knew was that I didn't have a father or mother and half of my siblings were gone. No one ever tried to explain any of this or how, as a child, I was supposed to get through this. So, at the age of 10, as I was sitting in church during my father's funeral, all I could think about was that I couldn't depend on anyone else. That day I felt a change in me that would last for years. I made a commitment to myself that I would never ask anyone for help no matter what the situation might be.

When I visited my mother in prison I would always cry and try to think of ways to get her out. She had a blood disease and her health was failing. At least once a year she had to have a blood transfusion. In those days, white blood could not be given to a black person, so I would get together three or four of my friends from school and we would donate our blood for her transfusions.

After several years, when I was thirteen, I decided that I had to get her out of prison. She always told me that any white person with influence could get her out on parole, so I set out to find that person. There was a man named Mr. Branch who was the owner of a grocery store in a small town called Sidon. He paid me a little to pump gas from time to time. One day I got up enough courage to talk to him. I was breaking the promise I'd made to myself to never ask for help, but I wasn't asking for myself, so as he leaned over the counter looking down at me, I said, "Can you help get my mama out of prison?" My voice was cracking as I explained to him, the best I could, what had happened. He told me that he would think about it.

I went back to see him several times until he said he would do something. I never knew what exactly he did, but within four months my mother was released.

Locating an influential person and negotiating the release of my mother from prison was my first business deal.

After her release, my mother moved me, my younger brother, and two younger sisters to the small town of Greenwood, Mississippi. My five older siblings had moved to Chicago. She never mentioned my father or his death, and I never asked her about it. No one did. I suppose I didn't really want to know. Instead, I chose to be grateful that I had a strong mother who never gave up and instilled in me a strong work ethic. She was always busy and worked hard. She would sometimes work seven days a week cleaning other people's homes and taking care of their children. Even though we were on welfare, (we used to say that we were so poor that poooor had four o's!) my mother could take the monthly $40 that we received and pay rent and feed and clothe four of us children. She was a great example to me as to how you are to work and provide for your family.

She was also one of the smartest people I knew. She had many ways of encouraging me with words of wisdom: "Get a good education so you don't have to work in those cotton fields; Get good grades; No work, no eat; If you don't work, you'll steal; Learn to cook and clean house because you might marry a lazy woman; Always work hard and save money for a rainy day; Keep busy, because an idle mind is the devil's workshop; Select your friends carefully; Always wear clean underwear." (I'm still trying to figure that last one out.) There was one key thing she told me that I didn't adhere to. Always be truthful, she said. Don't be a liar, because when you tell one lie, you'll have to tell another to cover up the first one, and someday the truth will find you out.

I had a wonderful 8th grade teacher, Mrs. Robinson. She not only taught math, but life as well. She told us to read everything we could get our hands on and, even after we graduated and started working, to always check the want ads in the newspaper to see if there was a better job than the one we had. She believed in learning more than one skill. These pieces of advice were some of the things that put me on my life path.

High school was a time in my life that I really enjoyed. During my four years there I had a perfect attendance record; no matter what issues or problems I had, I would not miss school or be late. I wanted to be the best in my class. I ranked third out of my class of 95 students. There was a group of us who competed for the best grades because we all wanted to be honor students, and we were. I also wanted to be an athlete but I wasn't good enough so I settled for being the manager of the basketball team.

When I was 21, I married my high school sweetheart, Verdie. We were married for thirty years and had four boys together but, even with her, I was not able to talk about my father. It wasn't until I was in my 50s that my sister Adell and I finally talked about his death and I finally felt something free up within me.

The death of my father and my decision to love and honor my mother set the course for the direction of my life. For years I worked several jobs and went to college full time to make sure I was prepared to do whatever was necessary to become successful. I was always willing to work hard. The work paid off as things began to come together for me. I built a very successful property management company that had a great reputation. At one point I was responsible for 14 HUD-insured or HUD-subsidized apartment complexes throughout the Chicago area, totaling close to 5,000 units.

Then things began to fall apart. My wife Verdie and I divorced. Three years later, I married my second wife, Mia. My business seemed to be doing well, but I knew that there was a serious cashflow problem developing. Still, I felt like I had all the answers. My pride kept me from seeking advice or counsel from anyone. I wanted to be in control. To find shortcuts and quick answers in my business deals, I took "microwave" approaches. The more mistakes I made, the more I tried to cover them up. I stopped reporting important information to the government about some of the properties I managed. I even started creating false records to deliberately mislead authorities. I knew that a lie can't live forever, but I thought that I could be creative and the consequences wouldn't catch up with me. It was like I was on a road where detour signs were all along the sides, but I ignored them and kept going.

Proverbs 16: 18-19 tell us that "Pride goeth before the fall." Because of my mistakes and bad business practices, an investigation was launched by the U. S. Department of Housing and Urban Development's inspector general that would last almost five years.

This was the beginning of the end.

2 THE INDICTMENT

Every year my wife and I spent the last week of December in Jamaica on vacation. I was there when I got a call from one of my employees that one of my clients had called asking when I would be back. He was requesting all of his accounting records. This was the beginning of an investigation that would last five years.

A lawyer once told me that most people who go through this kind of situation usually go into a state of depression. This happened to me. As the investigation dragged on, I sank deeper and deeper. I got to the point where I couldn't think clearly. Making decisions at work became difficult. I didn't go out except to work or to church because I didn't want to be around people who would look at me strangely or ask questions. I started to dress differently, switching from my normal suit and tie to jeans and t-shirts. My wife was being pressured too. She worked for me and we also owned other businesses together. The investigators suspected her of being involved in my schemes. I felt helpless as I watched her go through questioning and public embarrassment that she didn't deserve.

This kind of depression is difficult because most people going through it won't admit that they are in this state. This was certainly true for me. I didn't see a doctor because I didn't want to appear to be weak.

The indictment against me came in June 2005. I was charged, along with two associates, with conspiring to defraud the U.S. Department of Housing and Urban Development of at least $995,000 over nearly nine years. It was published in the newspapers and I felt just like I did that day when I was 10 years old at my father's funeral. I felt lost and like there was no one I could talk with. It hit me so hard that I became almost mentally paralyzed. It was as if I was floating in the ocean and couldn't get back to shore because there was no one to throw me a rope or a life jacket.

Finally, in 2007, my sentencing hearing was set. As I prepared for this day, all I could think about was where I had come from, what I had accomplished, and all of the plans I had made while growing up in the Mississippi Delta. I was about to lose everything that I had worked so hard for, including money, investments, and reputation. Some of my so-called friends and associates ran from me. That's when I knew I was in big trouble. I soon realized that there are two types of friends, standers and runners. Standers are those who will stand with you no matter what. Runners are those who start running at the first sign of trouble. There weren't many standers. It kind of reminded me of an old joke about going into a roach infested house in the dark and when you turn on the light all of the roaches start running for cover. There were some that were brave enough to stay, or maybe they just got confused by the light.

Even my attorney ran. He had his associate call me the day before the indictment to tell me that they couldn't represent me anymore because I couldn't afford their services. All my bank accounts had been frozen, which meant that I had no access to any money. So I had to appear in court the next day with a public defender who advised me to plead guilty. He told me we would work everything out in a plea agreement. Then, ironically, that attorney was fired from the federal public defender's office for accepting money from a client. So I was appointed a new public defender, someone who was young, inexperienced, and new to Chicago. He met with me for about an hour and also told me to plead guilty. But I wanted to explain myself to the judge. I wanted him to know that my client, the Chicago Housing Authority, paid my company on a schedule that often put me 90 days in arrears and made it impossible to meet ongoing expenses. At one point I had even used $190,000 of my own money to cover payroll. I wasn't making excuses. I admitted that I had made a huge mistake.

"I know what I did was wrong," I said, "but it was not to intentionally hurt anyone. It was very bad business practice, and a way to keep cash flow for the projects."

I hoped the judge would consider house arrest. But he told me that sentencing guidelines limited his options. He said, "I feel like you are probably one of the most ethical people to appear in front of my court. But there's nothing I can do."

I was sentenced to four years in a federal prison. I was 64 years old. Because of the extreme pressure that we were under, my wife Mia filed for divorce; the papers arrived two days before I left for the United States Penitentiary in Marion, Illinois.

3 NO PLACE TO BE ME

Going to prison for four years is not something that you take lightly. I was scared, but I didn't know how to ask for help. I needed to find someone who could give me some advice on how to get through this without causing more damage. But I couldn't seem to do it. Even after all that had happened, I still couldn't get past the commitment I had made to myself when I was at my father's funeral that I would never ask anyone for help. So I tried to navigate through this phase on my own.

On September 30, 2007, my last day of freedom, I got up early to prepare for the 300-mile trip to Marion, Illinois. I knew this day was going to be tough. I kept thinking that this should not be happening to me at this point in my life. This was the time when I was supposed to be slowing down and enjoying my life with my family and friends. Mia was with me; the divorce papers had come in the mail just two days earlier, but I didn't know if she was really going to follow through with it. We still had a good relationship and I understood why she filed. The investigation had taken a toll on her, and she was also about to lose everything. This kind of pressure would create hardships on anyone, and it did.

One of my sons was there that day. I knew the last several years had been hard on all of them. They had trouble getting jobs in property management because of me, and one of my sons had moved to Orlando to get away from the scandal. They didn't ask any questions about where I was going or how I felt. We didn't talk about it, but every time I saw them I could tell that they were struggling. I didn't want them to worry about me. On that last day, I thought, "How do I show my family that I am not nervous or concerned about the unknowns facing me?"

These words came to mind: "I don't know what the future holds for me, but I know who holds my future." I repeated this several times to myself and it helped to calm my nervousness. I promised myself that I would keep my conversation light so we could enjoy the day.

After I got dressed I went out to the front yard to check on my flowers. I love flowers; they make a house seem alive. I watered them to make sure they would live for another two weeks or so. At about 8:30 a.m. our friends Rob and Bridgett arrived. They have been our closest friends for several years and agreed to drive down with us so that we could make this a fun trip.

We loaded up the car with their luggage. I had very little to take. I was only allowed to bring the clothes I was wearing, a pair of white gym shoes, one pair of blue jeans, and a white or gray jogging suit. We set off, and as we drove, we talked about where we would eat breakfast. We agreed to look for one of my favorite breakfast places, the Cracker Barrel. I ordered my favorite pancakes with blackberry topping, smoked sausage, and eggs over medium, with a side of sausage gravy.

Rob looked at me and said, "Billy, is this your last meal?"

We all laughed and I said, "I'm not taking any chances."

When we hit the road again, I decided to drive because it kept me from thinking about what I was about to face. We laughed and joked around a lot to keep anyone from getting depressed. After a few hours, we came upon this shopping mall outlet, so we decided to stop and do a little shopping. The problem with this shopping trip was that everyone else could buy things, but I couldn't because where I was going, I wouldn't need anything. But just having my close friends with me was a joy.

The camp I was assigned to is located in a small southern Illinois town. It, along with other prisons, constitutes a major industry and is one of the largest employers in the area. Once we arrived, we checked into our hotel, then decided to drive over and check out my new home. As you can imagine, this was not the highlight of the day. Trees blocked the view and we didn't see much of the camp, which was probably a good thing. I think I would have been more depressed to see it and be thinking about it all night.

For dinner, we chose a barbecue place next door to our hotel, then tried to settle down for the evening. For me it was an awkward night. Mia wanted to stay awake so we could talk and spend some time together. We drank several cups of coffee to help us stay awake, but we were just mentally drained.

Before Mia turned out the light, she wrote me a note that said, "Bill, I don't know what to say. What should I do? This is so hard. I still feel like I am in a fog, like this is not real. I don't want tonight to end."

I knew she was hurting. Whenever we had issues in our marriage she would leave notes. I held her and told her I felt the same way and the only thing we could do was to enjoy this time together.

As I laid in bed that night, a song came to mind. The lyrics were "I must have done somebody wrong," by Little Willie John, a blues singer from the 1950's. He sang about his troubles and that maybe they were the result of the way he treated somebody in the past. It made me recall some of the things I had done and the people I had hurt along the way, people I never apologized to or asked forgiveness from because of my pride. I thought I must also be paying for my past sins. What it came down to was that I must not be a good person.

I always thought that I was in control, that I had it all together and that I could do anything. Everything was about me and what I could do. I even had a street named after me. I had people who called on me for advice, and organizations that sought me out to serve on their board of directors. I had become the "go-to-guy" and I had made a lot of money.

With all this adulation and adoration, I became arrogant and prideful. It lead me down a road of destruction. There is a line in the song from the movie *The Fighting Temptations* that says "I went to sleep one night on the top of the world and I woke up with the world on top of me." That is precisely the way I felt. I had always been the one others called on to help solve their problems. Now I was faced with the challenge of a lifetime and I had no answers and no way out.

The next morning we woke up about 8 a.m. It was October 1, 2007 and I was to report to the prison camp at noon. We went to Bob Evans for breakfast, and afterwards we sat in the car and prayed. Rob was a minister, so he asked God to protect me and keep me safe. After all this, we still had time to spare. We drove into Marion and sat on the benches that lined the downtown square. It seemed that all of the people who drove by were older people. We made jokes but it was the most surreal slice of time I've ever experienced, waiting to give up a portion of my life for a dumb decision I made several years earlier. I kept assuring Mia and my friends that everything would be all right and that I would be okay, but that wasn't how I felt.

Finally it was time to head for the "federal resort" that would be my new home. The woman who was going to check me in met us in the parking lot. She was very kind, saying that I would be fine, and she allowed me to spend a few last minutes with Mia, Bridgett, and Rob. They all gave me farewell hugs and then drove away. As I watched them disappear I felt scared and alone, like a small child being dropped off at school on the first day. But I was 64 and so added to that was an even bigger fear: that I would die here. At that moment, I truly didn't think I would survive it.

As I walked in, I didn't know what to expect. I had heard about federal prison camps and had also done some research on the computer, but I couldn't find anything on Marion. Now that I was there, I understood why. This was no place to be somebody!

It seemed to be a place that time and the outside world had forgotten. The correctional officer (CO) on duty had a deep southern accent that reminded me of my days growing up in Mississippi. He made it clear to me that he was in charge as he searched every part of my body. As he did, he said, "Stay away from these young guys around here because you're an old guy from the big city and you can get caught up. Stay away from any illegal activity. Mind your own business and do your time and stay out of trouble and you'll be alright."

When I thanked him, he said, "Here, you can keep your Bible."

Next I was introduced to the camp clerk, who happened to be from my old neighborhood on the near north side of Chicago and went to high school with two of my sons. As he showed me around the compound and introduced me to the area where I would be sleeping, I saw all these faces of young black men and thought, "This is not the place for old men."

Very quickly I understood that the staff personnel were not here to help me or any of the other inmates. They were only there to make sure that we stayed in our places and maintained the status quo. Their attitude was that 80% would end up back in prison. It was just a job to them because, as I was told by my roommate, "Man, we're all just inmates and no one listens to or pays attention to inmates." Over time I would learn that they followed their own rules, not necessarily the rules of the Bureau of Prisons.

I saw men there who had a very difficult time dealing with being incarcerated. It seemed as though they had the weight of the world on their backs. I could see the expressions on their faces that seemed to say, "I can't make it" or "this isn't real" and "how am I going to get through this?"

The first several months of incarceration were very difficult for me too. There were two inmates to a room that had no door, so there was no privacy. I learned immediately that no one undresses in the presence of another inmate. I was required to keep my area clean, my bed made and take a shower on a regular basis. My roommate was named Sterling, from St. Louis. He was in his 40s and was convicted for selling drugs. He had served two years of a seven year sentence. I didn't know then that he would come to be a friend to me.

At first it seemed as though I was living someone else's life. I didn't even have a name initially. The other inmates called me O.G., which meant Old Guy. I fell into my own routine, which included walking every morning and playing racquetball or softball. Everyone had to work unless they were disabled. Most started out cleaning bathrooms, mopping hallways, or washing dishes. I was assigned a job in the library and was paid twenty cents an hour to file newspapers, magazines, and old books that had been donated. I worked about four hours per day, five days a week. Weekends were tough. Visitation was on Saturday and Sunday and though Mia did not come visit me often, she did begin sending $300 a month and continued sending that amount until my release.

For weeks I sat by myself in the chow hall so I could observe where people sat and how they ate. Finally I began to sit with other white-collar criminals just to see how they felt about things and what they talked about. None of them felt that they should be in prison, and that included myself. They also felt they should not be with drug dealers because they were not as bad as they were. When the crack cocaine laws changed in December 2007 some inmates got their sentences reduced and some were released early. This really caused problems with the white-collar guys because nothing was being done for us.

I had to pray a lot to get myself through this period of life. I would go from day to day worried about what was going on with my family back home and sad about all the things I was missing—the good life, so to speak—and planning what I was going to do when I got out. I worried about what people would think of me and if I would be able to restore or repair my reputation. I had a lot of time to think about what I had created for my family and myself. I was so focused on myself that I didn't think about anybody else and what they were going through. My wife Mia had struggled through this with me and so had my children. They had to deal with all of the negativity and the fallout from the mess that I had made. Mia had to defend herself against things that I had done and it took her three years to clean up the mess that I created for her.

I thought about all these things, things that had very little value, things that would only push a person into deeper depression.

From time to time, I received letters from friends who wrote that they knew it must be tough being locked up and that they felt sorry for me. One thing people should never do is to write these kinds of letters to individuals who are incarcerated. When you're behind those walls, you want to hear encouragement. You want to get through it without negative stuff from outside. It's different when others who are inside talk about how tough it is. They can say it, but it can't come from the outside. Inmates would rather hear that the family is good, that they are praying for you and hope you're doing well. Any sympathy or pity is like pouring water on a drowning man. I took those kind of letters and filed them in the permanent file.

I struggled like this for a few months until it hit me like a punch to the face; If I continued this way, when I got out of here I would be a nut case. I realized that I had the answers to all of my problems lying right there on my desk and that was the Holy Bible. For years I had read it on and off, but never quite got into it the way I should have because I always thought that I had all the answers. That's what pride will do to you. Pride will never let you believe you are wrong and it will make you think you are stronger than you are and keep you from seeking help when you need it. It's the worst form of disease, one that most people don't think they have until it's too late. And if it's not treated it will destroy you. This I know from experience.

One day I was sitting on my bed trying to meditate and the word "peace" came to me. All I could think about for that day was "peace." I looked up Philippians 4:7. "And the peace of God, which transcends all understanding, will guard your hearts and your minds in Christ Jesus." I started crying. Until that point it had been a daily struggle, and all I wanted was this kind of inner peace.

My roommate said, "Mr. Moorehead, what's wrong with you? What you crying about?" As people got to know me, they had started calling me Mr. Moorehead, except the guards, who called us a lot of names, but never used the word Mister.

"Nothing," I told him, and I found myself smiling.

Peace came. I never worried anymore after that. God had granted me peace and things began to fall into place. I could sleep at night. I could talk to people, I could eat, and I could stop worrying about things I couldn't control and what I was going to do when I got out. I stopped worrying about my family.

I developed a new attitude. People began to see a difference in me and they started asking me why I always seemed to be happy.

"Why are you smiling all the time?" they asked. "You're in prison too!"

They wanted to know if I was going home soon. I told them that I had prayed about being delivered, and I had gotten the peace that I needed to move on. I started meeting with about 10 other inmates every Friday night for a Bible study. Here I was able to share what had happened to me, and talk about the new peace that I had found. My heavy load was gone.

That's when I knew I would survive this time at Marion.

4 POPULATION

When I arrived at the camp on October 1, 2007, the population consisted of 305 men. The racial breakdown was about 75% black, 20% white, and 5% Hispanic. The average age of the inmates was under 50.

In this camp there were basically two types of criminals: white-collar and drug-related criminals. White-collar criminals are those who have committed financial crimes or fraud. Drug-related criminals are those who dealt with the unlawful sale of drugs.

The white-collar criminals (which included me) were about 90% white, whereas the drug-related criminals had a more complicated twist: about 70% of them were black, 10% Hispanic, and 20% white. The majority of blacks were incarcerated for crimes related to the sale of cocaine or crack cocaine, compared to the whites who were there for drug sales or for the production and sale of methamphetamine.

The question that came up from time to time was, "Who are the worst criminals, the drug dealers or the white-collar criminals?" This question was never settled. We only knew that we were all there and we were all treated the same.

The socialization between the racial groups was the same as on the outside: the blacks stayed to themselves, whites to themselves, and Hispanics to themselves. And the sleeping arrangements were also assigned according to race. Even though from time to time I saw a black and white inmate assigned to the same bunk area, at mealtimes, in the cafeteria, each group would stick together.

This separation was common throughout the camp, from TV watching to the workouts on the weight pile. Despite the separation, or maybe because of it, there was very little racial tension. We all somehow managed to get along. Eventually we realized that there were no special privileges, no matter where you came from or what your status was on the outside. Any one of us could be assigned to cleaning bathrooms.

A large percentage of the population was uneducated, guys who never finished high school and who had been involved in illegal activities for most of their lives. It was a requirement of the Bureau of Prisons that this group receive GEDs while they were incarcerated, but that policy was never enforced. So these men left worse off than when they came in. The majority of them would not sign up for classes that could improve their lives. They just didn't see the need to do so.

There were the bodybuilders who spent hours each day working out, no matter how cold or hot it got in the outdoor workout area. They never missed a day, nor would they change their schedule no matter what else was going on. There were the weak-minded who wanted to fit in and were easily co-opted into the underground system and into criminal activities with other inmates. There were the gangs, who were responsible for most of the unlawful activities, including bringing contraband in from the outside.

There were the white racists who operated as a covert group. Their racism showed subtly through their quiet conversations, their off-the-wall remarks, and their demeanor. They acted as if they were superior to the black inmates and thought they should be treated differently. No matter what crimes they had committed, they felt that they were not as bad as the blacks they had to live with. This really came out when Barack Obama was running for president. They were still having trouble even after he won. This included the staff. They played it off as conservatives versus liberals. And this attitude didn't come just from men from the small or southern towns, but also among the whites from all parts of the country, which is a sad situation in this day and age. I had to ask, "Is this typical of white mens' thinking or is this just the thinking of the men here?"

There were people with serious mental problems who should have been someplace where they could be treated. There were some who had serious physical health issues who should have been receiving healthcare someplace else. This was especially true in the elderly population, which included me. For elderly inmates, socialization was limited because we couldn't play basketball or lift weights (which was the most common activity), so we were stuck with walking the track, watching TV, or playing cards or dominoes. All these activities, except walking, I considered "brain dead" so I participated in activities that would keep me healthy, which most elderly inmates did not do.

I saw several elderly inmates struggle to survive. There was an 85-year-old man named Carol who was there for not paying some federal taxes, and his wife died while he was in prison. Tardy was a 70-year-old homeless man with a drug habit who had sold guns to finance his habit. A former city councilman from a town in Alabama was convicted for accepting nine hundred dollars in campaign contributions, and he died of a heart attack within three months of being incarcerated. There were others with debilitating conditions who could not walk.

Over a two-year period, I personally witnessed a major increase in the elderly population and people in ill health, both physically and mentally. I wondered why people like this were incarcerated. It has to be very expensive, considering the health costs.

5 DRESS CODE

As inmates, our dress code required that we wear green uniforms Monday through Friday from 7:30 a.m. to 4:00 p.m., so during the day we all looked alike. During off hours we were allowed to wear gray sweats or gray shorts. Often you would see men wearing gray shorts over their long sweat pants. On other occasions some wore two pairs of sports shorts under their sweats and three T-shirts. I have no idea what this represented or accomplished and no one could explain it to me.

One of the fads in the camp was oversized clothing. The average young man under the age of 40 wore his clothes at least two sizes too large. It had no special meaning. It was just the style.

Another style was wearing pants below the butt. I was told that this was once a signal gay inmates used to let other inmates know they were available. There were a lot of guys wearing their pants low, so I assumed that times had changed and this look was now in fashion. Still, I tried not to sit in a chair that these guys had been sitting in because you never knew what was going on or going around. I had to protect myself and my health.

Do-rags and caps were another big deal. A lot of the blacks used do-rags, but I saw a few white guys and Hispanics wearing them also. This was because they all wanted the wave look. On top of the do-rag they wore wool caps to seal in the moisture. Some men even slept in these wool camps, whether it was winter or summer. This was something else that no one could explain to me. It was just something they felt comfortable doing.

6 FOOD AND MEALS

The food they serve in these places is atrocious. For breakfast we usually had grits, oatmeal, or bran flakes with stale donuts or coffee cake. Never any meat. Usually the bran flakes were as tough as cardboard because they had been stored in the warehouse for too long. This institution never discarded anything; some food had expiration dates of more than three years. Lunch always included beans, no matter what else they served. There was seldom any fresh food, and no fresh vegetables of any kind except hot peppers in the summer when there was a garden. Once a week they served baked chicken that was so old that it was black on the inside. They also had chicken patties and fish patties (or as some called it, fish bread). On Wednesday they served stale hamburgers with fries.

I lost 30 pounds in the first six months.

Some of the inmates would act like children, particularly at mealtimes. On weekends there were twice-a-day counts, at 10:00 a.m and 4:00 p.m., and that was close to eating time. When the count was over, men would break and run for the cafeteria as though they were going to miss out on something. It was a sight to see grown men running for food. They complained about the quality but always ate everything on their trays and also what anyone else would give them. There were inmates who never seemed to get full, no matter what the food tasted like. They would start lining up at least thirty minutes before they started serving and would get in line more than once. Before one meal was finished they were asking about the next. After dinner they started microwaving their snacks and this could go on until midnight. They cooked whatever they bought, stole, or borrowed. And this was a daily routine.

Many inmates developed a strange habit: they ate from bowls because there were no plates available outside of the cafeteria, so they would carry their bowls with them wherever they went. I joked with them that when they got home they would be walking around their houses with their bowls in hand, looking for food.

If you had health problems and were in need of a special or healthy diet you were in the wrong place. There was no such thing as a healthy diet. If you ate this food every day there was no way you could leave without some health problem, particularly if you were elderly or had a health issue when you came in. Inmates who had served time at other places said that the food was slightly better at some other places.

For me, the food was so badly cooked and tasted so awful that I could hardly eat it, and I wasn't the only one. Every day it seemed that half of it was put into the garbage.

7 LANGUAGE AND CONVERSATION

To sit and talk to inmates, whether it was in a group or individual setting, you would think that there was no such thing as a dumb prisoner. These guys knew everything. The majority of them thought they had the answers and the solutions to the world's problems, which made me wonder how they ended up there in the first place, and who made the mistake.

There is a saying, "a fool is considered wise until he opens his mouth." When they opened their mouths all kinds of things came out. This wouldn't have been a problem if their opinions didn't have such influence on others. Some of these guys had been in the system several times and for many years all they had known was crime. They had these warped ideas and they influenced younger people who were just entering the system, as well as the weak-minded who were already in the system.

I seldom got to know inmates' correct names, particularly those who had been there for a long time or in more than one institution. Most inmates take on a new name or nickname or want to be known by their initials. Nicknames usually reflected where they came from, how mean and tough they were, their size and height, how cool they were, how smart they were, and how old they were. They had names like OG, Pops, Big Slim, GI, Hen Dog, Peps, Pee Wee, and Q.

They seemed to think that the more profanity they used, the bigger the person it made them. Or that the one who cursed the loudest won the discussion. They began most sentences with the F-word and every third word was also the F-word. These kinds of conversations went on all day, no matter who was around, and the topics never changed. They talked about basketball games they were playing or had played, or about their daily soap opera or something they were watching on Black Entertainment Television. To them this was very important stuff. One group hung out in the Situation Room, an area set up during the presidential elections where we watched CNN or Fox, and they considered themselves to be among the intellectuals on the compound.

I had a real problem with the use of the "N" word by the black guys and the "M-F" word by all of the guys. Whenever I engaged in a conversation with someone who started using those words, I would remind him that when he had a conversation with me I would rather he refrain from using profane language. As time went on, most of the guys began to show me the respect that I requested. When they got out of line, and they did from time to time, I would remind them with a line from Maya Angelou that I felt was very appropriate: "When you use profanity it's an ignorant mind trying to express itself." This would always leave the guys looking for a comeback.

If I could overlook the cursing, some of the conversations were thought-provoking and in most cases interesting, whether political or racial. Sometimes they would get out of hand and someone's feelings would get hurt, but it didn't matter. The conversation would keep moving right along.

You could tell a lot about a person by his conversations. You could determine who would be back in prison and who wouldn't, or who would merely survive on the outside and who would be successful. If I listened closely they would usually tell everything about themselves.

I think it's the male ego, or maybe pride, that makes us want to talk as if we are an important person. Our conversations reflect who we think we are or who we want to be, particularly when we are around other males. Being in a prison makes that more apparent; you feel you always have to be a tough guy. You can't be a softy, especially in a camp.

A lot of the men had had bad experiences with females, so when they talked about women, conversations would be laced with the "B" word, and worse. Some seemed downright angry. It really showed whenever anything came on TV about female abuse. These guys would find ways to justify why a woman deserved to be abused or beaten. Many had probably been in an abusive relationship and would probably be again because of their complete lack of respect for women.

One topic that seldom came up was family. Very few inmates talked about their families and their support. Some had not seen or heard from family members since they'd been incarcerated. Others had been written off by their families because they'd been in and out of prison so many times.

8 CAMP ACTIVITIES

A prison camp is nothing more than a warehouse of men. It provides nothing positive in the way of rehabilitation, nor does it prepare anyone for the outside world. If you were not a good person when you went in, odds are you will not be good when you get out. There were so many negative activities that in most cases it was like being on the street, only on a smaller scale. Illegal activities included gambling, drugs, alcohol, theft from the kitchen and warehouse, and smuggling in contraband from the outside. Some men said it was better being behind a fence, or higher security prison, where there was more discipline and less temptation. There were those who couldn't deal with too much freedom.

Television watching is a major activity in all institutions. It has practically become an art form. At Marion, there were 13 televisions and they all had to be specially assigned by stations and programs in order to avoid disagreement about what to watch. There were TVs assigned to Black Entertainment Television and NASCAR because the inmates who watched these programs were diehard fans and they would become very upset it they couldn't watch their programs. These two groups were very different from one another. The B.E.T. group was made up of young urban blacks and the NASCAR men were whites of all ages, mostly from small towns, rural areas, and the South. TV watching was taken so seriously that if someone changed the station without a group vote there could be a fight. It was common for men to get up to watch TV at 6:00 a.m. and stay up until 1:00 or 2:00 a.m. the following day.

Television watching on weekends was a special treat; that's when movies were shown. Inmates prepared for movies as though they were going on a picnic or a major outing. They set chairs out around midday and prepared their food and snacks. It was a major event and they wanted it to be like going to the movies on the outside.

The other major event was the Super Bowl. Inmates started preparing for it at least a week ahead of time. On the Saturday before the game they started preparing their food. On that Sunday morning they started cooking early because everything had to be cooked in the microwave. By afternoon there would be tables of food. It almost looked as though a caterer had been hired and we could nearly imagine we were at home.

Gambling was another major activity in the camp, from dominoes to poker. Games were played seven days a week; they started immediately after the four o'clock count and could last until midnight. There was a lot of "money" changing hands; they played for postage stamps or racked up huge debts that were paid off with items from the commissary or stolen from the kitchen or warehouse. The inmates who became addicted to gambling couldn't afford it, and this habit usually led to more criminal activities. It was amazing how much was stolen to pay gambling debts. And unfortunately most inmates carry the habit home with them. What begins as a pastime in prison becomes something altogether different and more serious on the outside.

Oddie was a white guy from Iowa who loved to gamble and would bet on anything. I mean *anything*. He never got any respect from either the white or black guys. Whites didn't like him because he associated with the black guys, and the black guys didn't like him because he owed a lot of them money.

I liked Oddie because he was real, never showed any prejudice toward anyone, and showed me respect, even when I made it clear that I wouldn't get involved in anything illegal.

Sports were another favorite pastime, and were used as a means to keep things under control. Most of the inmates were young and black; they loved to run up and down the floor and fantasize about how great they were or how great they could become. They also had the weight pile where they could go and build their bodies, but they were never encouraged or counseled to go to a class to build or renew their minds. Sports were available an average of four hours a day, seven days a week, compared to roughly eight hours per week for limited education programs, like GED classes or correspondence courses.

For about six months I had a roommate named Jones. He was a 38-year-old black man who had been in prison for ten years and only had a high school education. Jones was very smart and was taking courses to get his associate degree. He was one of the best math teachers I have ever seen. He was also fluent in Spanish and was able to teach the Hispanic men. He was an exception. Of the total 300 inmates in the camp, only about 40 men were able to be enrolled in programs to become certified in things like heating, ventilation, air conditioning (HVAC), plumbing, electrical, or water treatment. That left 260 inmates who were not involved in any kind of meaningful activity. They were only being warehoused.

How can this change anyone?

Because there was no emphasis put on education or helping us become better or more productive people, I concluded that they didn't want us to become too smart because we might start questioning the way the system works, or I should say, *doesn't* work.

9 RACISM

Racism runs deep in small communities, and most prisons are located in small white communities. The people who live in these communities are not used to diversity. They have never had any relationship with minorities other than keeping them locked up in prison. Prisons have become the major industry in some of these areas and they employ a lot of local people. Often these employees reveal their racist attitudes in the way they do their jobs and the way they relate to the black inmates.

When Barack Obama was elected president the correctional officers took his picture and copied it on a food stamp. They hung it where the black inmates could see it, saying that it was the new dollar. This was to let us know what they thought about being black. We knew if they didn't respect the president of the United States, they definitely weren't going to respect black inmates.

Some of the inmates reminded me of my days growing up in Mississippi during the 1940's and 50's. There was Ray, an ex-state representative from Tennessee. We arrived at the camp on the same day. He had such a deep southern accent that whenever we had a conversation I would ask him to repeat himself. Ray and I talked a lot. We were both Christians and went to church services and Bible study together, but he was a bit strange when it came to black people. He thought that most of us were inferior to whites. He would make blatant racist statements and not even realize that what he said offended anyone. Some of the black inmates asked me why I even talked to him. I had never had a chance to talk to someone like Ray and I wanted to understand where he was coming from and why he felt the way he did. Through my conversations with Ray I began to wonder if he was really racist or if he just didn't know any better. Sometimes he was a decent guy.

Then there was Little John, a white guy about my age who often watched the national news with me. He would analyze and critique how President Obama was performing. John told me that he grew up in a household where his parents hated black people and that he had never associated with black people until he came to prison. All of the guys knew John's situation and, for whatever reason, no one held it against him.

From talking to inmates who had been in other institutions, I learned that racism seems to be a major problem throughout the system. As the system grows, the problem continues to get worse because the people being hired are still coming from these small communities. Racism is so deeply rooted in these small towns that it makes it impossible for it not to overflow into the prisons. No one will address the issue from the top and if inmates try to address it from the inside there is some type of retaliation. If someone files a written complaint it takes such a long time to get a response, and then it's sent back to the warden, where it usually dies.

I want to make it clear that I am not painting everyone with the same brush. There are some good people working at these institutions but there are a great number who have this racist attitude.

10 UNDERGROUND ECONOMY

There is a saying inside that goes, "Mind your business and do your bit." I learned to not talk too much and stay away from illegal activities. Even though it seemed that someone was always watching, there were guys who never stopped hustling. If they could steal something, they would steal it and sell it to other inmates for cash.

Because Marion is a low-security prison camp, there are no fences around the perimeter, just signs to mark the boundaries of the property. Certain guys would make arrangements with other guys on the outside to leave contraband in the woods behind the grounds, everything from cell phones, iPods, cosmetics, clothing, food, vitamins, cigarettes, to tobacco, booze, and drugs. Body-building protein drinks were an especially popular item. I would see guys coming into the building with bags of stuff, but I did as I was told and minded my bit. These lifetime criminals, as I called them, figured out how to avoid the security cameras and the guard who drove a truck around the grounds. If anyone was ever caught, he would be transferred out of the camp.

The most popular places to work were the kitchen and warehouse because there was more of an opportunity to steal there. The longer these guys worked in these places the more aggressive they became. They developed an entire economy in order to get services that weren't provided by the Bureau of Prisons. They even set up small "stores" that they operated from their area. Their biggest sales came from snack food, but in this underground economy it was possible to buy anything you wanted or needed. And I mean anything.

The illegal stores were not cheap; they usually charged from two to three times what the items were worth. In addition to using cash, we could buy things with postage stamps. If an inmate had no way to pay at the time, he was given credit until he got paid or he got money put in his account from the outside. Then he was given a list of items that he had to return to the store man. This was a continuing practice, and even though it was in violation of camp policy, it served a purpose and met a need because the quality of the food that was served in the chow hall was so bad.

Even the commissary, where we were supposed to buy the things we wanted, was one of the greatest rip off joints of all times. It was worse than any store that you would find in the worst ghetto in a big city. The food sold there had little or no nutritional value. It was all junk food and it was all overpriced. I was careful about what I bought there because a lot of the items were outdated.

Clothes and gym shoes were also sold in the commissary, but they were usually irregulars and were are also overpriced. You could go to any Walmart or Sears and buy the same clothes for half the price.

On average, an inmate would spend $200 per month in the commissary for inferior food and clothes because we couldn't legally have any of these items sent in from the outside. Our jobs paid only 12-40 cents per hour, so a lot of swapping and trading was done as well. A common practice was to make a deal with other inmates to provide services like washing and ironing clothes or bed linens, shining shoes, mopping floors, typing, or tutoring. One person provided the necessary service and the recipient then cooked food and shared it, or bought things from the commissary in exchange for the services.

11 HELP FOR INMATES

Inside the prison camp, there was very little help in the way of education or counseling for social problems. There was drug counseling on a limited basis, but none for any major issues that could arise in an inmate's life. A lot of the guys lost touch with their families once they arrived. Many, like me, ended up divorced. It was a very lonely, isolated time and there weren't many places to turn for support. There was one full time chaplain on staff, but he also had to cover the maximum security prison across the street, so his time was very limited.

In order to adapt to prison, it's important to find someone to talk to and trust. There are all kinds of things going on inside these places: drugs, alcohol, tobacco, and other things. Sometimes I got the feeling that I was on the streets. As someone who had never been incarcerated, finding a buddy was a way to learn the ropes. I relied on my roommate Sterling for support. We prayed for one another and prayed for our families. Sterling loved God and knew the Bible well. He had almost every spiritual reference book imaginable so he could always support his beliefs with Scripture.

He and I had our disagreements. When we did, we would let each other cool down for a day or two and we'd be back to being Christian brothers. We always tried to practice what we were teaching. With Sterling and the other men from my Bible study, I was able to learn so much more about God and how to live my life.

There was a young man we called G.I. because he was from Gary, Indiana; he adopted me as his father. G.I. always tried to protect me from harm. He became my protector. He monitored me while I exercised to make sure I wouldn't overdo it, since I had a tendency to push myself to the limit. Sometimes G.I. would even cook for me or come by my room to make sure I had eaten. Every night he would check to make sure I was in bed. I remember one Saturday night when I had chest pains and they had to call the doctor, G.I. sat outside the clinic until midnight to make sure I was okay.

I felt sorry for the men who didn't have a good support system, or who let themselves be taken advantage of because they thought that was friendship. If an unscrupulous person got information about you, he may try to exploit you. You had to be very careful about what you told others. You always had to keep in the back of your mind that they were in prison for committing a crime and that you were not dealing with Boy Scouts.

Some inmates had trouble with socialization because of mental issues. I could spot those with bipolar disorder or other issues. They struggled with self control and unfortunately didn't get much help. There were staff members with job titles like "Case Manager" and "Counselor" who had no experience helping inmates with their problems, nor did they seem to want to help. Worse, it seemed that if the correctional officers showed that they wanted to help they wouldn't be around long. They could get transferred because the unspoken agreement was that they were there to keep us in prison, not to show that they cared or that they were sensitive to our problems.

With so many men coming through this system and so little support for them, it's no wonder they go back on the streets and commit additional crimes.

12 MEDICAL CARE

The quality of medical care in this institution was some of the worst that I have ever seen. I base this on my experience serving as the chairman of the board of a community health center for 22 years.

When I arrived, the doctor gave me a partial checkup and said to continue taking any medication that I brought with me. There was no discussion about why I might need to take medications. The doctor ordered a blood workup as standard procedure, but I was never told if there were any problems. There were inmates who had health issues such as high cholesterol, high blood pressure, Type II diabetes, and other sicknesses but were never told, so they didn't know to make adjustments in their lifestyles. Inmates leave prison in bad health, not even knowing their conditions, and as time goes on their health gets worse, creating more problems for them and their families.

One of the reasons health care is so bad in prison is the attitude of the medical staff. From my understanding, it is difficult to find people who like working in this types of setting. Therefore, the people who are attracted to work here are not the best. That was really the case at the camp. They seemed to always have a bad attitude, which made us afraid to ask questions. Most men would choose not to follow up to see a doctor if they had any recurring problems.

There was no dental care at all. The only thing that was provided was a quick exam. If someone needed a tooth pulled they would take care of that, but nothing more. There are men who have been in prison camp for years and have never had their teeth cleaned.

Eye care was almost as bad. They allowed inmates to have their eyes examined by an optometrist for glasses, but they never allowed an examination by an ophthalmologist for infections or disease. If an inmate had any serious eye problems he was out of luck and made do until he got out or got worse; usually it was the latter. The optometrist was not a staff position, but an outside contractor retained by the prison. Because of this, it took from 90 days to six months to get the results of examinations.

There was no mental health care at all and mental problems are a big issue in all institutions. There are people with serious mental problems who should not even be in prison. They should be sent to a place where they can get the help they need so they will be able to function when they get out. These men are taken advantage of by others and coerced into doing illegal things while they're incarcerated. They also have problems getting along with others and are quick to get into fights because of serious anger problems. Depression is also a serious problem that could be handled by assigning a mental health counselor or providing individual counseling, but it doesn't happen.

Healthcare in prison should be just as important as healthcare on the outside. A healthy prison population will save the government money and save lives, but somehow this is not an important issue. Inmates are looked at as scum who need to be punished. The administration doesn't seem to be concerned about the welfare of people who don't contribute positively to society. What they don't realize is that at some point someone will have to pay. An inmate takes his bad health wherever he goes. If healthcare is not dealt with properly it can cause major problems in outside communities.

For example, there was a man named Earl who was overweight, had high blood pressure, major heart problems, diabetes, and over a period of years developed major kidney problems. If his earlier problems had been dealt with appropriately, it's possible that his heart and kidney problems would never have developed. Because this did not happen, Earl ended up being sent to a major medical facility to receive dialysis.

This kind of thing is not out of the ordinary. Healthcare was a low priority unless someone was close to dying.

13 RELIGION

All prison systems have a chaplain and organized religious services each week, but there are so many religions represented that the chaplain can't address them all. At Marion, there were at least a dozen different organized religions, plus those that had been created by the inmates. I'm sure that in larger institutions there are many more.

Sometimes this created a problem about who got the attention. "How do we all get treated fairly?" was the question. Inevitably some were left out. On the other hand, there were also inmates who went to all the services. I guess they wanted to make sure they were covering all bases. To me it seemed like they just ended up more confused about what they believed.

There were also outside prison ministries that came in on a regularly scheduled basis. They brought much needed spiritual support to those who believed in God. This was particularly true for me. As a Christian who was used to being part of a fellowship and attending church services on Sunday and Bible study on

Wednesdays, these ministries helped to keep me grounded and connected to what God expects from me as a man.

For the younger guys especially, these ministries played a vital role. They didn't have anything positive going on in their lives, or anyone they could depend on for spiritual support. A lot of them had never been involved in any form of religion. Being in prison gave them an opportunity to explore this side of themselves, something they wouldn't have done on the outside because of the activities they were involved in.

Often the inmates would lead religious services. These services varied based on who was in charge and how large the group: Baptists, Catholics, Muslims, or Jehovah Witnesses. The largest number of men were Christian.

Some of the problems that came with inmate-organized services were some of the teachers and preachers and their beliefs. In some cases these self-taught individuals didn't quite understand what they were teaching and preaching and they misled people who wanted to change their lives. In some cases these people could be very convincing and they sounded good.

I was disturbed by the large percentage of individuals who used religion for the wrong reasons. Many were serious about positive changes in their lives, but others used it as a way to run a con game on their families, loved ones, and anyone else that they could benefit from. They were smart, cunning, and knew the right words to use.

They could quote Scriptures that would make you think that they were changed. When they called home or got visits from family or loved ones, they talked the language of religion to impress whomever was listening and as a way to get what they wanted. All the time they were scheming. Once they get back on the street the real person shows up, this time with all he learned in prison. Usually it's not good.

Most inmates used religion to help them meet their objectives, whatever those were. I guess they were no different than people on the outside. It seems like a lot of people are doing the same thing these days.

Still, there were truly good guys who gave their best. They sometimes got a bad rap and were lumped together with those of us who relied on our genuine faith to get by. The guys who were faking it made it more difficult for people to trust any of us who were religious. I often felt I had to prove myself.

One way I put my faith into action was to witness to other inmates whenever possible. There was this older guy I'll call Mr. B. who was about four years older than I was and we lived in the same area. Mr. B was an atheist and had been in prison for more than twelve years. He felt that he had to portray a tough guy image and he did this partly by using the "M-F" curse word constantly. It bothered me and Mr. B knew it.

One day I sat down and had a long talk with him about his language and why it offended me. I explained that I was a Christian and that this language disturbed me. I asked him to control himself. It didn't work entirely, but it did work most of the time, and I was then able to talk to him about God and the Bible. He would listen intensely, then usually go off about the fact that there is no such thing as God, and anybody who believed in that stuff was crazy. But I never gave up. I planted the seed and hopefully God will water it.

14 BECOMING PART OF THE SYSTEM

I knew that I could not allow prison to become a part of me. Too many men let themselves develop bad habits and ways of talking that proves to be a turnoff to their family and keeps them coming back. A lot of men tried to fit in by getting tattoos. Some got their whole bodies tattooed. I didn't know exactly what this meant or what it represented, but I think it has to do with their masculinity and showing how tough they are. Many also grew beards or long hair or both. It seemed as though they were trying to disguise themselves. It may be that they were hiding from who they had become—a criminal. To most, this was tough to live down.

On the other hand, there were people who enjoyed being there. There were young men who preferred it to being at home. They could stay up all night and sleep all day. They could play basketball whenever they wanted to or go to the weight pile and work out any time of the day. They didn't have to worry about doing any hard work or going to school because there was no pressure to do so. They got three meals a day whether the food was good or not, and they had a place to sleep. To use an old expression, some of these guys were happy as a kid in a candy store. I heard comments like, "Why should I want to get out? I'll only have to worry about paying bills and finding a job."

But being in prison strips you of your identity. You have to redefine who you are and what you stand for, and you must make it known. Otherwise you become what someone else wants you to be.

Once you enter this system, it doesn't matter what you were on the outside. You're just an inmate. There are doctors, lawyers, bankers, chefs, businessmen, drug dealers, young and old, you name it. Once reality sets in you realize that you have become a nobody. You are just like everybody else, with no special rights. You have left all of that on the outside. You have to prepare yourself to live by all of the rules, without any special privileges. You come to be defined mostly by where you are assigned to sleep or your job assignment.

White-collar criminals had a harder time accepting this. When they were on the outside they lived respected lives and in most cases contributed to their community. They came to prison thinking that they should be treated with the same respect that they received on the outside. They didn't want to face up to the fact that the crimes they committed were still crimes.

Some inmates accepted who they were and where they were, but others continued to parade around as though they were in a make-believe world. There was this one ex-politician from

Tennessee who I talked to from time to time. He had the idea that he was "somebody" and could not understand why he was not treated with the same respect he was used to getting. He wanted to socialize with the correctional officers, even though he was reminded several times by staff that he was nobody special. He could not get it in his head that he was just another inmate. He had been in prison for over two years and it still had not sunk in.

There was a so-called bishop of some church organization who thought he was the spokesman for all of the inmates, especially the black inmates. He appointed himself as a spokesman and tried to convince the inmates that he was a very important person. Every morning he would go to the gym and set up his office to meet with his "disciples," who were convinced that he was an ordained bishop in the Church of God in Christ. He had branched off and started his own church and ordained his own elders to go out and start their own churches and ministries. Somehow he thought this elevated him to a level of importance. It didn't work. Most of the inmates thought he was a nut case, and the staff just didn't care.

There were a number of such people who came in and out of this system, mostly white-collar criminals, who didn't quite get it. I saw professional people who could barely function on a daily basis, some who were doctors and lawyers on the outside. They could barely get out of bed. Or they would sleep only three or four hours a time at night. This pattern usually went on for a long time, at least until they learned how to deal with it. Some did and some didn't. Some could never get over the frustration that came from trying to prove to others that they were somebody.

I realized that I felt somewhat the same. I didn't want to admit it because of my pride, which has always been a problem for me. Pride, ego, and shame were a constant struggle. *Pride,* because I felt that I had always been "the man," that I had all the answers and no one could tell me anything. I never sought advice; it had to be my way. *Ego,* because I thought that it was all about me. I was self-centered and didn't know how to reach out. This forced me to feed on self-pity and if I wasn't careful, that's where the deep depression would come in. *Shame,* because I felt I let a lot of people down, particularly my family and loved ones. I worried about how my children were affected. Had I become a nobody in their eyes? Then I began to worry about what other people in my community or those I worked with would think about me. The more I thought about this the guiltier I began to feel.

One man told me that he felt ashamed because his parents were ashamed of him. They would not tell people where he was and they would not visit him. I know that some families deal with the shame by moving to a new community where they are not known, hoping to get a new start. We all have to find our own ways of dealing with our issues.

15 THE INJUSTICE SYSTEM

The justice system is supposed to be fair, equitable, and impartial in the treatment of competing interests and desires of individuals with regard for the good of all. Somehow this has gotten lost. I know from experience that there is very little fairness in this system. There are individuals who commit the identical crime in different parts of the country or even in the same city. They end up with totally different sentences. There are unscrupulous prosecutors who want to make a name for themselves who will do anything to win a case, including lying and cheating. The strange thing about this is that it is lawful for them to lie to you, but it is illegal to lie to them. Is that fairness?

Plea agreements are another issue; an individual waives his right to an appeal, essentially giving up the only right he has if he discovers a mistake or malfeasance committed by his attorney. Judges approve of these agreements knowing full well that most individuals have no idea what they are giving up. A person has almost no recourse to correct the injustice and the system has no fair way of dealing with such issues.

Because I worked in the law library, I got a chance to talk to a number of people who had given up their rights through a plea bargain. They had no idea what they had done and their attorneys never explained to them that they were waiving their rights. In most cases these men had never read their agreements until they came to prison. All they wanted to do was get through the crazy system. And crazy it is.

Another injustice is lawyers who sell their clients short for expediency's sake. Not a single inmate I talked to liked his lawyer or the way he was represented. This was not because they felt that they were innocent, but because they all believed that they were sold out and given bad advice. More than 95% of inmates had pled out of their case. This resulted in a lot of angry people who felt shortchanged.

One lawyer described prosecutors as "bloodsuckers." I thought that was an unusual description coming from another lawyer, but many inmates would agree with the label. Whether right or wrong, all attorneys seem to want is a conviction. They will destroy families and innocent people in the process. This is justice at all costs, but at what cost?

At some point there will be negative results. You simply can't lock everybody up. Although that seems to be the trend; prisons are one of the fastest growing industries. They employ thousands of people, they have strong union support, and they are located in mostly small communities where they are the largest employer. They are like McDonald's, which you very seldom see closing or going out of business.

Yet they produce no product or goods or services that can be sold to consumers. Prisons serve only as warehouses for people. Eventually what you store in a warehouse will spoil or rot. If you don't have a good system for moving items out of the warehouse you can end up with an overcrowded space, and that's what has happened with this prison system. Except we're not talking about products or items, but people. Can you imagine being a company that has over 75% of its product returned? If a company's performance was evaluated based on these figures, it would get a failing grade.

What does this tell us? It tells us that this system that is setup to punish people is broken and needs fixing.

16 CAN THE SYSTEM CHANGE ANYBODY?

Prison was originally established to rehabilitate, but that changed. Now the belief seems to be that people can be punished into doing the right thing. The prison mentality is, "What do I need to do to survive?" Inmates immediately go into survival mode. Whatever that is to them is what they will do. Most of the time they don't think about the consequences and they don't understand that they'll take the bad habits they develop with them when they leave.

Prison breaks a person's spirit. The longer a man serves, the harder he becomes. He has little feelings for others and doesn't understand what relationships mean. So rather than rehabilitating men, prisons are creating better criminals, or at the very least, people who have a tough time making it once they get out.

My observations as an inmate, plus my research and interviewing of inmates who have been in other institutions, show that the biggest failing of the system is that it doesn't do enough to prepare people for the outside world. Prison officials and employees believe that it is not their job to do this. As a result, some people go in and can never get out.

I met men in their twenties, thirties, forties, and even fifties who had been there since they were in their teens. This was not a small number. The recidivism rate was more than 75% and the disheartening part was the large percentage of young black males. I believe that this is by design.

Prisons are simply not organized to produce anything good. When you are imprisoned it's very difficult to remain the same. You either become better or worse. Most men come out angry because they feel they've been given a bad deal or had bad legal representation, angry about overzealous prosecutors who wanted to win at all costs without considering fairness, and angry at prosecutors who sometimes act worse than the criminals they are prosecuting.

Mostly they are angry because they feel abandoned. I saw good men come in who seemed to change overnight. They became so depressed that they could not function and there was no one to help them. If a man was married when he came in, it was likely that his spouse would divorce him. I heard a lot of men talk about friends they had on the outside and how they all disappeared. Guys would say that you really find out how many friends you have when you get locked up. It was rare to hear an inmate talk about getting a visit from a friend. Of the men I talked to who had been in prison more than twice, nearly all their families had given up on them. Without family or friends to support you, how can anyone make it?

For any good to come out of this system it will have to change. There are too many young people entering these places with no means to prepare them for a better life. Too many are being incarcerated for petty crimes that could be better addressed through community service. This alone would save taxpayers so much money.

But the general public doesn't understand, or maybe doesn't care, about the magnitude of the problems as long as it doesn't affect them directly. And as long as people believe that the penal system does what it's supposed to be doing it will continue to play a role in destroying people's lives.

The Bureau of Prisons, and the justice system overall, needs to examine itself. It must begin with the prosecution, through how and where a person serves his time, to what kind of rehabilitation services he will need in order to avoid returning to prison. The people who run this system must find ways to control the growth. It's not something that politicians want to address because of the negative feelings about crime and criminals, but someone must address it and address it soon.

If I could advise the young men being incarcerated today, I would tell them that it is possible to make it through and come out better than before. I would say the same thing the correctional officer said to me on my first day: stay away from negative people and negative activities. I would say get involved in positive activities, things that will improve your life. Be willing to be transformed by the renewing of your mind. It all starts with the mind. And I would say do what has to be done to mend and rebuild relationships with family and loved ones. If you know who you are and know what you want, and if you want to accomplish something positive, you can come out a stronger person. You can be changed for the better.

17 THE LAST DAYS AND THE HALFWAY HOUSE

During my last days in the prison camp, I wanted to understand what had happened to me and the people that I met along the way. I didn't want my "education" to be wasted. One thing I can say is that I met both good and bad people at the prison camp.

As a Christian, I wanted to reflect Christ in my life. Some would say that I committed a crime and I went to prison, so I must not be a Christian. But I never stopped being a Christian, and tried to follow Christian values even while in prison. I will leave judgment up to God.

One of the most difficult things for me to deal with and understand was seeing all of the young men already in the system, as well as the number of new ones entering it. As fast as they would leave, they would be replaced and the revolving door never stopped. These were young men between the ages of 20-35. A number of them had been in the system most of their adult lives and the saddest part was that a majority of them would never make it out.

As I was leaving the Marion facility, they were shipping more and more young men into the camp, usually people with less than ten years remaining on their sentences. Marion was nothing more than a warehouse situation. It had too many inmates with nothing to do except watch television all day, seven days a week, twelve months a year. With no jobs and very few training programs they found other ways of entertaining themselves by gambling, weekend drinking parties, and other illegal activities. It reminded me of some of the neighborhoods back in Chicago.

Above all, my experience showed me that this was no place to be somebody. I saw firsthand how prison breaks men's spirits, if they weren't already broken when they came in. The last three months of my stay, my roommate was a white man named Joe. Joe was in his late 50s. He had owned two mortgage companies and was convicted of fraud. He was being sued for $58 million dollars and told me, "If I have to be poor, I think I'll commit suicide."

Joe had never been poor and didn't think he could adapt. I told him to strengthen his faith by praying and sharing with other inmates.

"That's the way out," I said. "Change your thinking."

Many men wanted to give up, just like Joe. I won't say that only the strong survive, but I will say that, in my opinion, the meek have a greater chance. In prison, just like on the streets, people take meekness as weakness when in fact it is the total opposite. In this case meekness means being focused and preparing oneself to go and do positive things. The so-called "strong" men that I met were dead set on going back and doing the same things because they thought they had all the answers.

My first roommate Sterling was an example of someone who was strong in faith. He read a lot of Christian books and became a resource for others. He was one of the few guys whose wife visited every single weekend. That was unusual. He wanted to make sure he deserved her commitment and vowed to be the best husband he could be. He was released, got a job, and supported his wife and child.

As the time came for me to leave the camp and transition to the halfway house, I became excited. I was eager to return to Chicago and a new environment. I didn't realize that the population I was about to be part of was the same as the one I was leaving, maybe even worse.

In the halfway house there were a lot of men from different federal prisons with no self-discipline who felt they were free and could get away with anything. Some of them violated all the house rules and were still on their way to being released back into the community.

Don't get me wrong. I'm not against the halfway house concept. But these men needed to be better prepared and counseled on how to live. They had anger that had built up over the years and they had very little respect for people, women in particular. Some had mental health issues that had not been addressed. How could they hope to have a smooth reentry? By the time they reached a halfway house, it was almost too late.

18 WHAT THIS EXPERIENCE TAUGHT ME

As I go through life, I remind myself to stop and think about who I am, what I have become, and ask, "Am I the person God wants me to be?" I make myself write down the answers to these questions and review them from time to time so I don't get off track.

I know people might argue that crime is a moral issue, but I believe it is deeper than that. Most men coming into the system have a multitude of problems and the Board of Prisons is not equipped to deal with them all. I often thought that if they could invest the money they put into cars and trucks into programs that would assist inmates, they would better prepare men to reenter society. I was grateful that I was in a position to make it through.

I believe God allowed me to have the time away so I could think about my dreams and how I pursued them. I had to learn that life is about more than having money and power and acquiring material things. My life had reached a point where I never had enough. I had to work harder to make more money to buy more stuff, which led to shortcuts, increased pressure, and resulted in mistakes being made.

Despite my mistakes, I learned that God never left me. He did not run from me. He stayed and got me through all of it, even when I thought I would not make it to the age of 65. There were times when my faith was weak, but God had my back and this kept me going. I was able to experience the peace and joy that can't come from other people. Once I knew that, I knew that I could overcome any problem.

I have had to let go of the burden of guilt I felt about taking my family to jail with me, so to speak. They suffered, even though they were not physically behind bars, because they had to deal with the negativity of the incarceration. Not one of them ever asked me what I did that led to my arrest. I believe they thought that whatever I did was so bad that they didn't want to know. They read about it in the newspapers and heard about it from other people. But none of them ever heard the complete truth from me.

God never promised that life would be easy. Even though I've paid for my crime, I know I'll continue to deal with negative treatment. There will always be a stigma around being an ex-offender, even within my close relationships. Sometimes even loved ones can seem ashamed of being seen in public with me, or not want others to know that they are associated with me. Some people, when they see me in public, try to avoid me or have a quick conversation before rushing off in a hurry. As I make my way through this life I've made a decision to not allow the way people treat me to affect the way I treat them because then I give them a power and control over me that they are not entitled to. This is a conversation I've had often with other inmates. We all knew we would be treated differently; we just did not know how badly.

Finding employment will always be difficult for me because of trust issues. But I understand that I broke the line of trust on my own, not because someone forced me. Sometimes I remind myself what the judge said to me at my sentencing: "Mr. Moorehead, you are one of the most ethical people to come before my court. I wonder if anybody will ever hear or read that."

Standing before the judge, I thought about that moment, 54 years earlier, when I sat in front of the pastor at my father's funeral and made that promise to myself to never depend on anyone. It was a promise that took me off course, but the judge's words lifted me, and I wished my father could hear them. Instead, I've learned to turn to the grace of my heavenly Father. Despite the challenges that lay ahead for me, I know I've made it through with God's help, and I am at peace.

I am truly a blessed man.

ABOUT THE AUTHOR

William Moorehead is a graduate of DePaul University with a degree in Urban Studies. He worked as a social worker for fifteen years before becoming an owner of a successful property management company and developer of low and moderate income housing in Chicago. He was also involved in organizing a community health center in Chicago that provided healthcare to the underserved.

68152176R10049

Made in the USA
Lexington, KY
03 October 2017